You Were

MADE FOR THIS

MOMENT

*HOW THE STORY OF ESTHER INSPIRES US TO
STEP UP AND STAND OUT FOR GOD*

STUDY GUIDE PLUS STREAMING VIDEO
FIVE SESSIONS

MAX LUCADO

WITH ANDREA LUCADO

HarperChristian
Resources

You Were Made for This Moment Study Guide
© 2021 by Max Lucado

Requests for information should be addressed to:
HarperChristian Resources, 3900 Sparks Dr. SE, Grand Rapids, Michigan 49546

ISBN 978-0-310-13625-5 (softcover)
ISBN 978-0-310-13626-2 (ebook)

Any internet addresses (websites, blogs, etc.) and telephone numbers in this study guide are offered as a resource. They are not intended in any way to be or imply an endorsement by HarperChristian Resources, nor does HarperChristian Resources vouch for the content of these sites and numbers for the life of this study guide.

HarperChristian Resources titles may be purchased in bulk for church, business, fundraising, or ministry use. For information, please email ResourceSpecialist@ChurchSource.com.

First Printing July 2021 / Printed in the United States of America

Contents

Introduction

Winter casts a cold shadow. The days are short. The nights are long. The sun seems shy, hidden behind the grayness of the days. Warmth has packed her bags and migrated to the tropics. Beach weather would be nice. But that's clearly not going to happen anytime soon.

Winter brings danger. Blizzards. Ice storms. Broken pipes and slippery sidewalks. Caution is the theme. Come springtime, and you will run barefoot through the meadow and plunge into the pond. But now? It's best to button up, zip up, stay in, and stay safe.

Is it winter where you are? Are you trapped in a perpetual gloom? Has life not turned out the way you thought it would? Maybe your finances fizzled. Or your health never recovered. Or a friend never returned. A Siberian cold has settled over your life.

This study was born in winter—a pandemic that locked down the world. Church doors closed. Students were stuck at home. Masks hid smiles. And in the midst of this trial, an ancient sin threatened to undo us: *racism*. An officer's knee on the neck of a black man activated a subterranean anger. A volcano of rage spewed into the streets of most countries.

Many have wondered if this winter season would pass. Perhaps *you* have wondered if its lingering effects would ever end. If so, God has a six-letter word of encouragement for you: E-S-T-H-E-R. The book that bears her name was written to be read in wintertime. It was crafted for those who feel outnumbered by foes, outmaneuvered by fate, and outdone by fear.

It's almost as if God, in his kind providence, heard all our prayers and said, "Follow me. I want you to see what I can do." He escorts us now to the front row of a grand theater and invites us to take a seat. He nods at the symphony conductor, and all at once the music begins, the curtain opens, and we are eyewitnesses to a masterpiece of divine drama.

The characters of this drama comprise a complex and colorful crew. There is Xerxes, the clueless brute of a king. Haman, the egotistical and bloodthirsty right-hand man who plots to exterminate the entire race of the Jewish people. Mordecai, a Jewish man himself, who realizes he cannot compromise and must take a stand. Esther, our main character, gorgeous and gutsy.

And God . . . well, where is God in this story? Even though the fate of the Jewish people—his chosen people—is at stake, at no point do we read "God said," or "God chose," or "God decreed." There is no mention of the temple or the name *Yahweh* or *Elohim*, the Hebrew nouns for God. Why the seeming silence from the Almighty?

Certainly, God has been known to intervene dramatically in Scripture. By his hand the Red Sea opened, the manna fell from heaven, a virgin gave birth, and a tomb gave life. Yet for every divine shout there are a million *whispers*. The book of Esther relates the story of our whispering God, who in unseen ways superintends all the circumstances for his people. This priceless book reminds us that God need not be loud to be strong. He need not cast a shadow to be present. He is still eloquent in his seeming silence . . . and active when he appears distant.

The theme of the book of Esther—and indeed, the theme of the entire Bible—is that all the injustices of the world will be turned on their head. Grand reversals are God's trademark. When we feel as though everything is falling apart, God is working in our midst, causing everything to fall into place. He is the King of quiet providence, and he invites you and me to partner with him in his work. For each of us has a part to play in his grand drama.

The headline of the book of Esther reads: *Relief will come.* But the story also reveals that God will call us at times to walk onto the stage, step into the spotlight, and take bold risks to make that relief come to pass. He will raise us up "for such a time as this" (Esther 4:14). The question is not whether *God* will act . . . but whether *we* will step out in faith when he does.

How to Use This Guide

The *You Were Made for This Moment* video study is designed to be experienced in a group setting (such as a Bible study, Sunday school class, or small-group gathering) and also as an individual study. Each session begins with a brief opening reflection and questions to get you thinking about the topic. You will then watch a video with Max Lucado, which can be accessed via the streaming code found on the inside front cover. If you are doing the study with a group, you will then engage in some directed discussion and close with a time of prayer.

Each person doing the study in a group should have his or her own study guide, which includes video teaching notes, Bible study and group discussion questions, and between-sessions personal studies to help you reflect and apply the material to your life during the week. You are also encouraged to have a copy of the *You Were Made for This Moment* book, as reading it alongside the curriculum will provide you with deeper insights and make the journey more meaningful. (See the recommended reading section at the end of each session for the chapters in the book that correspond to the material you and your group are discussing.)

To get the most out of your group experience, keep the following points in mind. First, the real growth in this study will happen during your small-group time. This is where you will process the content of the message, ask questions, and learn from others as you hear what God is doing in their lives. For this reason, it is important for you to be fully committed to the group and attend each session so you can build trust and rapport with the other members. If you choose to only "go through the motions," or if you refrain from participating, there is a lesser chance you will find what you're looking for during this study.

Second, remember that the goal of your small group is to serve as a place where people can share, learn about God, and build intimacy and friendship. For this reason, seek to make your group a "safe place." This means being honest about your thoughts and feelings and listening carefully to everyone else's opinion. (If you are a group leader, there are additional instructions and resources in the back of the book for leading a productive discussion group.)

Third, resist the temptation to "fix" a problem someone might be having or to correct his or her theology, as that's not the purpose of your small-group time. Also, keep everything your group shares confidential. This will foster a rewarding sense of community in your group and create a place where people can heal, be challenged, and grow spiritually.

Following your group time, you can maximize the impact of the course with the additional between-session studies. For each session, you may wish to complete the personal study all in one sitting or spread it out over a few days (for example, working on it a half hour a day on four different days that week). Note that if you are unable to finish (or even start) your between-sessions personal study, you should still attend the group study video session. You are still wanted and welcome at the group even if you don't have your "homework" done.

This study is intended to help you gain new insights into the character of God and recognize some of the ways that he might be working "behind the scenes" on your behalf. So, as you go through this study, be listening for what God is saying to you as it relates to your current season, be watching for the subtle ways that he is moving in your midst, and be ready and willing to "step into the spotlight" when he calls you to act.

Cozy in the Culture

ESTHER 1:1–2:18

WELCOME

The middle school lunchroom. Do you remember the place? Plastic trays, mystery meat, mini-milk cartons, soggy potato chips . . . and you. You're a twelve-year-old kid who has just made it through the lunch line and is now standing, tray in hand, looking over a sea of students and strangers who have already managed to group together at the tables. The question overwhelms you. Perhaps it even kept you up the night before. *Where will I sit?*

All you want as a twelve-year-old is to *belong.* And at that age, to belong means to *fit in.* You don't want to stand out from the crowd, or be perceived as a loner, or have people think you are in any way strange or different. You want to fit in . . . even if it means compromising.

Fortunately, for most of us these middle school years are long behind us. But unfortunately, this *"where will I sit?"* feeling doesn't end with the eighth grade. The desire to fit in, and doing whatever it takes to do so, lingers well into our adulthood.

In this first session, we are introduced to Esther and Mordecai, the stars of our play. Eventually, they will also prove to be the heroes of our tale. But they don't start off that way. When we first meet them, they are fully assimilated into the Persian culture that their families have been a part of for three generations. They have Persian names, work for the Persian government, and live in the Persian city of Susa, one of the kingdom's main hubs.

As Israelites, Esther and Mordecai had been called to be a holy people who were set apart for God. As Christ followers, we are called to be the same. We are, as Peter said, to see ourselves as "foreigners and exiles" in this world (1 Peter 2:11). Life isn't supposed to feel too cozy. After all, Jesus has called us to do uncomfortable things—such as believe in him when those around us do not, and love our neighbor when our neighbor is hard to love, and share his grace and hope with others even when we are afraid of how they may react.

As we turn the pages of Esther, we find that Esther and Mordecai had a great call on their lives—a seemingly impossible task set before them—and that they rose to the occasion. But we can't forget they started out a bit skittish and hesitant. Yet this fact should give each of us hope, for if God can use them to do great things in spite of their desire to compromise and conform to the culture, then he can certainly use us to do great things as well.

SHARE

If you or any of your group members are just getting to know one another, take a few minutes to introduce yourselves.

Then, to get things started, discuss one of the following questions:

- What do you already know about the book of Esther? How do you respond to the idea that Esther and Mordecai didn't start off as all that heroic?

— *or* —

- In what season of life does this study find you? The gloom of winter? The hope of springtime? Something in between? Explain your response.

READ

Ask one person to read the following passage, and then discuss the questions that follow.

Do not conform to the pattern of this world, but be transformed by the renewing of your mind. Then you will be able to test and approve what God's will is—his good, pleasing and perfect will (Romans 12:2).

What does it mean to conform to the pattern of this world?

How does conforming to the pattern of this world prevent us from knowing God's will?

WATCH

Play the video segment for session one (see the streaming video access provided on the inside front cover of this study guide). As you watch, use the following outline to record any thoughts, questions, or points that stand out to you.

God has given us a role to play in the grand drama we call life. There will be times when he will call us to step onto the stage to perform the part that he has designed for us.

Mordecai and Esther were members of the Jewish race—the exiled descendants of the people of Israel. There are many words we could use to describe the Israelites, but above all they were to be *holy*. Biblically, this meant they were to be set apart.

Mordecai was three generations removed from the first Jerusalem exiles. He had begun to assimilate to the Persian culture and blend in rather than stand out. He had gone clandestine with his convictions and deferred his theology to the bureaucracy.

The compulsion to compromise affects us all. Everything around us says "conform." Our society permits all beliefs except an exclusive belief. It says it's okay to do whatever you want as long as you accept what everyone else does.

To believe in Jesus as the only redeemer is to incur the disdain of Persia. This is why we must remember our *true* identity. Our eternal citizenship is not the one printed on our passport. We are subjects of a different King.

We have the same mandate as the Israelites—to be caretakers of God's promise. The message of Jesus has been entrusted to us, and we have the hope the world needs.

DISCUSS

Take a few minutes with your group members to discuss what you just watched and explore these concepts in Scripture.

1. How would you describe Xerxes based on what you have heard about him so far?

2. How would you summarize the events that led to Esther finding herself in the position of becoming the next queen of Persia?

3. Read Leviticus 19:2 and Deuteronomy 18:9. What does *holiness* mean in these contexts? What was God calling his people to represent in the world?

4. Review Esther 2:5–11. What clues are we given in this passage that reveal both Mordecai and Esther were conforming to the Persian culture?

5. Thank about a time you were tempted to assimilate to fit in with the culture. Share that experience. How did it affect you? How did it affect your faith?

6. As Christ followers, we are all called to be holy, or set apart, for God. What does holiness look like as a follower of Jesus?

RESPOND

Use the space below to describe someone whose life indicates he or she is working toward holiness. How do you know this about that person? What do you admire about him or her?

PRAY

Close your time in prayer. Ask God to help you see any ways that you might be conforming to the culture around you, and ask him to empower you to start taking bold risks for him. Write down any prayer requests the group has, and pray for those needs during the coming week.

Personal Study

*I*f you haven't already started reading the *You Were Made for This Moment* book by Max Lucado, now is a great time to begin. This week, read chapters 1-3 before doing this personal study. The questions and exercises provided in this section are designed to help you receive the greatest benefit from reading the book as you apply it to your own life. There will be time for you to share your reflections at the beginning of the next session.

DAY 1: HOLY WHAT?

We often associate the word *holiness* with perfection—almost like a halo around someone's head. This can make the call to be holy feel like a very tall order. However, in Hebrew the word translated *holy* is *qadowsh,* which can simply mean "set apart." When we view it that way, the call is not to be perfect but to remain faithful to the path that God has set for us, which at times will set us apart from the culture. In this way, each of us can work to be holy. As Christ followers, it is not our own goodness or good deeds that make us holy, but rather the work of Christ on the cross. Keep these thoughts in mind as you read the following passages.

> ¹ *The* L*ORD* *had said to Abram, "Go from your country, your people and your father's household to the land I will show you.*
>
> ² *"I will make you into a great nation,*
>   *and I will bless you;*
> *I will make your name great,*
>   *and you will be a blessing.*
> ³ *I will bless those who bless you,*
>   *and whoever curses you I will curse;*
> *and all peoples on earth*
>   *will be blessed through you"* (Genesis 12:1–3).

> ¹ *The* L*ORD* *said to Moses,* ² *"Speak to the entire assembly of Israel and say to them: 'Be holy because I, the* L*ORD* *your God, am holy.*
>   ³ *"Each of you must respect your mother and father, and you must observe my Sabbaths. I am the* L*ORD* *your God.*
>   ⁴ *"Do not turn to idols or make metal gods for yourselves. I am the* L*ORD* *your God.*
>   ⁵ *"When you sacrifice a fellowship offering to the* L*ORD*, *sacrifice it in such a way that it will be accepted on your behalf"* (Leviticus 19:1–5).

1. What comes to mind when you hear the word *holy*? Where do you think this belief or association came from?

2. What promises did God make to Abraham in Genesis 12:1–3?

3. What instructions did God give to the Israelites that would set them apart?

4. What do these verses tell you about what it means to be holy and chosen by God?

Prayer: *God, I know that you are holy and that your holiness cannot be matched. But I also know that through Christ, you have made me holy. I am a part of your family, not because of any good deeds I've done, but because of the work Christ did on my behalf. You have called me to be set apart. Help me become more holy. Refine me, guide me, and teach me so I look more like you each day. Thank you for choosing me as yours.*

DAY 2: CAST OF CHARACTERS

In this session, we were introduced to three of the main characters that will be featured in our story: Esther, Mordecai, and King Xerxes. Even though the book of Esther is an ancient story from the Old Testament, we can easily relate to these characters, their flaws, their courage, and their trials. King Xerxes had incredible wealth and incredible power, yet he was self-involved and insecure. Esther and Mordecai were members of the Jewish race, set apart by God, and yet had fully assimilated into Persian culture. They even had names that honored Persian gods! Read the following passages that describe these characters and then answer the questions below.

> [2] *At that time King Xerxes reigned from his royal throne in the citadel of Susa,* [3] *and in the third year of his reign he gave a banquet for all his nobles and officials. The military leaders of Persia and Media, the princes, and the nobles of the provinces were present.*
>
> [4] *For a full 180 days he displayed the vast wealth of his kingdom and the splendor and glory of his majesty.* [5] *When these days were over, the king gave a banquet, lasting seven days, in the enclosed garden of the king's palace, for all the people from the least to the greatest who were in the citadel of Susa* (Esther 1:2–5).

> [5] *Now there was in the citadel of Susa a Jew of the tribe of Benjamin, named Mordecai son of Jair, the son of Shimei, the son of Kish,* [6] *who had been carried into exile from Jerusalem by Nebuchadnezzar king of Babylon, among those taken captive with Jehoiachin king of Judah.* [7] *Mordecai had a cousin named Hadassah, whom he had brought up because she had neither father nor mother. This young woman, who was also known as Esther, had a lovely figure and was beautiful. Mordecai had taken her as his own daughter when her father and mother died* (Esther 2:5–7).

⁸ Esther also was taken to the king's palace and entrusted to Hegai, who had charge of the harem. ⁹ She pleased him and won his favor. Immediately he provided her with her beauty treatments and special food. He assigned to her seven female attendants selected from the king's palace and moved her and her attendants into the best place in the harem.

¹⁰ Esther had not revealed her nationality and family background, because Mordecai had forbidden her to do so (Esther 2:8–10).

1. When you think about yourself and people in the Bible, do you feel similar to them, different from them, or somewhere in between? Explain your answer.

2. According to Esther 1:2–5, and based on what you learned in this session, what do you know about Xerxes? How are you different from him? How might you be similar to him?

3. According to Esther 2:5–10, what do you know about Mordecai and Esther? How are you different from them? How are you similar to them?

4. Why do you think God allowed flawed characters like Xerxes, Mordecai, and Esther to be in the Bible? What does this say about God and how he feels about you?

Prayer: *Heavenly Father, thank you for your Word. I know that every story in this book has a purpose. When I read about Mordecai, Esther, and Xerxes, I find hope in the fact that you can use anyone, no matter his or her own shortcomings. This gives me hope that you can use me too. I am flawed. I am a sinner in need of grace. But in Christ, I have that grace. And in Christ, I can be used for a greater purpose. Thank you, Lord, for making this possible.*

DAY 3: HIDDEN IDENTITY

Esther and Mordecai had chosen to create a world of hidden identity. They were now several generations removed from the first Jerusalem exiles, so it's fair to say they had at least partly forgotten their roots. Of course, while it's easy to judge them for hiding the fact they were members of God's chosen people, it can be just as easy for us to deny our own upbringing, family, or faith. If something threatens our ability to belong, we tend to compromise. It's instinctual . . . but it isn't holy. God called the Israelites to be set apart, and he has called us to be set apart in Christ. Keep this in mind as you read the following passages.

¹ As for you, you were dead in your transgressions and sins, ² in which you used to live when you followed the ways of this world and of the ruler of the kingdom of the air, the spirit who is now at work in those who are disobedient. ³ All of us also lived among them at one time, gratifying the cravings of our flesh and following its desires and thoughts. Like the rest, we were by nature deserving of wrath. ⁴ But because of his great love for us, God, who is rich in mercy, ⁵ made us alive with Christ even when we were dead in transgressions—it is by grace you have been saved (Ephesians 2:1–5).

¹³ Therefore, with minds that are alert and fully sober, set your hope on the grace to be brought to you when Jesus Christ is revealed at his coming. ¹⁴ As obedient children, do not conform to the evil desires you had when you lived in ignorance. ¹⁵ But just as he who called you is holy, so be holy in all you do; ¹⁶ for it is written: "Be holy, because I am holy" (1 Peter 1:13–16).

1. Why do you think the desire to fit in with others is so strong?

2. How does Paul describe in Ephesians 2:1–5 your way of life before you met Christ?

3. Peter urges you in 1 Peter 1:13–16 not to conform to the "evil desires you had when you lived in ignorance." What are some ways that you have seen God transform your life and move you toward his holiness? How has this work he has done helped you not to compromise your values or fall into the trap of conforming to the world's standards?

4. In what areas of your life do you struggle with conforming? How do these verses encourage you to ground yourself in Christ rather than feel the need to conform?

Prayer: *Heavenly Father, help me not to conform to the ways of this world. Renew my mind so that I may be transformed and know what is your good, pleasing, and perfect will. I was once dead in my sins and transgressions and satisfied the desires of my flesh, but you met me in that moment. You did not bestow wrath on me, because you are rich in mercy. Now I am dead to my transgressions and alive in Christ! I am so grateful for the work you have done within me.*

DAY 4: MADE FOR THIS MOMENT

It likely was difficult for Esther to believe there was a greater purpose for her becoming queen. For all she knew at this point, she had simply won a beauty contest. She didn't know that she had been made for such a moment as this. (She will shortly!) In the same way, it can hard for us to believe that we've been made for this particular time in our lives—that we've been placed here in this moment by God. Perhaps life feels like winter to us. It's difficult and dreary. Or maybe it's simply boring and mundane, and a sense of godly purpose is far from our everyday lives. But God has created each of us to live for such a time as this, as the following passage relates.

> ⁴ *As you come to him, the living Stone—rejected by humans but chosen by God and precious to him—*⁵ *you also, like living stones, are being built into a spiritual house to be a holy priesthood, offering spiritual sacrifices acceptable to God through Jesus Christ . . .* ⁹ *you are a chosen people, a royal priesthood, a holy nation, God's special possession, that you may declare the praises of him who called you out of darkness into his wonderful light.* ¹⁰ *Once you were not a people, but now you are the people of God; once you had not received mercy, but now you have received mercy* (1 Peter 2:4–5, 9–10).

1. Do you ever doubt if there is a greater purpose for your life? Why or why not?

2. What words does Peter use in this passage to describe God's people?

3. What have you been chosen for collectively as a follower of Christ?

4. Is it easy or difficult for you to believe that you are "chosen," a part of a "royal priesthood," and "God's special possession"? Explain your response.

Prayer: *God, I know you have chosen me as your child. Because of your mercy, you have made me holy, even though I am not deserving of holiness. I confess it is hard for me to accept your mercy and your love. I feel as if I need to earn it . . . yet I know I fall short. Help me to believe in today's passage. Help me to embrace and accept your mercy and love so I can live as if I am truly your special possession, treasured by you, full of your grace. Help me to believe this about myself so I can extend this same grace and mercy to others. In Jesus' name. Amen.*

For next week, read chapters 4–5 from *You Were Made for This Moment.* Use the space below to note any key points or questions that you want to share at your next group meeting.

A Moment of Decision

ESTHER 2:19–4:17

WELCOME

It was William Shakespeare who wrote, "All the world's a stage, and all the men and women merely players." We all play many different roles in life. But most of us haven't received what the world would consider a *leading* role. We aren't presidents, politicians, famous actors, or even Instagram influencers. We're just us—moms, dads, friends, sisters, brothers, corporate workers, teachers, servers, or carpenters. Most of us will never achieve Babe Ruth-level greatness. But that does not mean we weren't made for a purpose!

In this session, we will witness a critical turning point for our lead characters, Mordecai and Esther. As we have seen, up to this point they have been content to exist under the radar in the foreign culture of Persia, hiding the fact that they are members of the exiled Jewish race. But now, they will be faced with a crisis—what we might call a "Mordecai Moment" and an "Esther Event—that will cause them to act. They will come to a moment of decision where they must choose to stand up, step out, and take a bold risk of faith for God.

While you may never be a leading character as the world sees it, these same "Mordecai Moments" and "Esther Events" will come into your life . . . and often when you least expect them. God will orchestrate events in such a way that you will be compelled to move out of your comfort zone, make the decision to trust in him, and then take the steps as he leads. Perhaps you will be confronted with an injustice that causes you to speak up. Or you will encounter a needy person and be prompted to help. Or you will find yourself in a situation where you can share the hope you have found in Christ with someone who desperately needs the gospel.

Could it be that God has placed a specific situation or circumstance before you today? Could it be that you, like Esther, are at the right place at the right time for a specific purpose? If so, take heart from these words of Mordecai, challenging yet true: "Who knows but that you have come to your royal position for such a time as this?" (Esther 4:14).

SHARE

Take some time to share at least one key takeaway or insight you had from this week's personal study. Then, to get things started, discuss one of the following questions:

- When was a time that you felt compelled to confront an injustice (large or small), help a person in need, or speak truth into someone's life? Explain.

— *or* —

- Who is someone you admire for standing up for his or her beliefs? What about that person's actions has specifically inspired you?

READ

Ask one person to read the following passage, and then discuss the questions that follow.

> "Do not think that because you are in the king's house you alone of all the Jews will escape. For if you remain silent at this time, relief and deliverance for the Jews will arise from another place, but you and your father's family will perish. And who knows but that you have come to your royal position for such a time as this?" (Esther 4:13-14).

When is a time in your life that you received encouragement or some tough love from another person just like Esther received here from Mordecai?

What was the result of that nudge? Why did you listen—or not listen—to this person?

WATCH

Play the video segment for session two (see the streaming video access provided on the inside front cover). Use the following outline to record any thoughts, questions, or points that stand out to you while you're viewing the teaching.

Mordecai had resolved in his heart to *never* bow before Haman. A crisis is no time to prepare an escape plan. The time to preprare to resist temptation is before it strikes.

Haman revealed himself to be a servant of hell. Satan hoped to use Haman to destroy the Jews, thereby destroying the lineage of Jesus.

Mordecai moments are occasions in which God invites us to join him in his work. They are instances in which our true allegiance is revealed.

Mordecai had opened a window and shed a divine light into Esther's world. "You are here for a reason," he said. "You were placed here on purpose for a purpose."

God is the one who placed you on this planet in this generation. He determined your birthdate, your nationality, and selected your neighborhood. What if he knew the world needed someone like you at such a time as this?

You were made to stand up like Mordecai. You have been called to speak up in this world like Esther. You have the opportunity to be a participant in God's divine plans.

DISCUSS

Take a few minutes with your group members to discuss what you just watched and explore these concepts in Scripture.

1. What events led to Xerxes naming Haman as his right-hand man?

2. Read Esther 3:1 and Deuteronomy 25:17–19. What is the significance of Haman's ancestry? What history did the Israelites have with the Amalekites?

3. Review Esther 3:2–4. How has Mordecai changed since we first saw him in session one? What do you think led to this change?

4. What was Esther's initial response to Mordecai's plea to talk to Xerxes about Haman's plan? What caused her to react in this way?

5. What was Mordecai's response back to Esther? What was he essentially saying to Esther? What was he helping her to see about God's plans for her life?

6. Have you ever had a moment like this when you decided to call out an injustice after initially hesitating to do so? What happened as a result?

RESPOND

Spend a couple of moments considering injustices in your own community. These could be at your school, in your neighborhood, or in your workplace. What have you seen others do to address these injustices? What are some things that you could do to address this need?

PRAY

Close your time in prayer, thanking God for putting you on this earth for such a time as this. Confess any times that you have failed to act when God has prompted you to take a stand, and ask the Lord to help you be the hands and feet of Jesus to a hurting world. Write down any prayer requests the group has, and pray for those needs during the coming week.

Reflect on the material you've covered this week by engaging in any or all of the following between-sessions activities. Each personal study consists of a passage of Scripture and reflection questions to help you dig deeper into this week's session. The time you invest will be well spent, so let God use it to draw you closer to him. At your next meeting, share any key points or insights that stood out to you as you spent this time with the Lord.

DAY 1: SIN AS OLD AS TIME

In this session, we were introduced to Haman, the villain in Esther's story. Haman was hired by Xerxes to be his right-hand man, look out for dissenters, and do the king's dirty work. Haman's ancestry is significant. He is a descendant of the Amalekites, who had a long history of hostilities against the Israelites, as the following passages relate. Haman is far removed from these ancestors who fought the Israelites as they were escaping Egypt . . . but he decides to fight the

Israelites in his own time by using his power to declare their extermination.

> [8] *The Amalekites came and attacked the Israelites at Rephidim.* [9] *Moses said to Joshua, "Choose some of our men and go out to fight the Amalekites. Tomorrow I will stand on top of the hill with the staff of God in my hands."*
>
> [10] *So Joshua fought the Amalekites as Moses had ordered, and Moses, Aaron and Hur went to the top of the hill.* [11] *As long as Moses held up his hands, the Israelites were winning, but whenever he lowered his hands, the Amalekites were winning.* [12] *When Moses' hands grew tired, they took a stone and put it under him and he sat on it. Aaron and Hur held his hands up—one on one side, one on the other—so that his hands remained steady till sunset.* [13] *So Joshua overcame the Amalekite army with the sword.*
>
> [14] *Then the LORD said to Moses, "Write this on a scroll as something to be remembered and make sure that Joshua hears it, because I will completely blot out the name of Amalek from under heaven."*
>
> [15] *Moses built an altar and called it The LORD is my Banner.* [16] *He said, "Because hands were lifted up against the throne of the LORD, the LORD will be at war against the Amalekites from generation to generation"* (Exodus 17:8–16).

[17] *Remember what the Amalekites did to you along the way when you came out of Egypt.* [18] *When you were weary and worn out, they met you on your journey and attacked all who were lagging behind; they had no fear of God.* [19] *When the LORD your God gives you rest from all the enemies around you in the land he is giving you to possess as an inheritance,*

you shall blot out the name of Amalek from under heaven. Do not forget! (Deuteronomy 25:17–19).

[1] *Samuel said to Saul, "I am the one the* LORD *sent to anoint you king over his people Israel; so listen now to the message from the* LORD. [2] *This is what the* LORD *Almighty says: 'I will punish the Amalekites for what they did to Israel when they waylaid them as they came up from Egypt.* [3] *Now go, attack the Amalekites and totally destroy all that belongs to them. Do not spare them; put to death men and women, children and infants, cattle and sheep, camels and donkeys.'"*

[4] *So Saul summoned the men and mustered them at Telaim—two hundred thousand foot soldiers and ten thousand from Judah.* [5] *Saul went to the city of Amalek and set an ambush in the ravine.* [6] *Then he said to the Kenites, "Go away, leave the Amalekites so that I do not destroy you along with them; for you showed kindness to all the Israelites when they came up out of Egypt." So the Kenites moved away from the Amalekites.*

[7] *Then Saul attacked the Amalekites all the way from Havilah to Shur, near the eastern border of Egypt.* [8] *He took Agag king of the Amalekites alive, and all his people he totally destroyed with the sword.* [9] *But Saul and the army spared Agag and the best of the sheep and cattle, the fat calves and lambs—everything that was good. These they were unwilling to destroy completely, but everything that was despised and weak they totally destroyed* (1 Samuel 15:1–9).

Satan's strategy was to eliminate the Israelites before they gained strength as a people, so he led the Amalekites to attack them shortly after their escape from Egypt.

How did God bring victory to the Israelites? What decree did the Lord make at that time?

2. What did Moses call the people to remember in Deuteronomy 25:17–19?

3. What command did God make to King Saul in 1 Samuel 15:2–3? What reason did God provide for instructing Saul to take these actions?

4. Why do you think Saul failed to obey this direct command from God?

Prayer: *Dear Jesus, thank you for your hand of protection over my life and over my family. I know that Satan desires nothing greater than to "steal and kill and destroy" (John 10:10). Thank you for being my Good Shepherd and for laying down your life for me. Continue to protect me from the enemy's attacks and help me to obey your instructions—without reservation or hesitation. Thank you for your forgiveness, mercy, and grace when I confess my failings to you.*

DAY 2: MORDECAI MOMENTS

Mordecai had his "moment" in this session. He revealed his true identity as a member of the Jewish race and stood up for what he believed in (literally) by refusing to bow before Haman. In session one, we witnessed a more passive Mordecai— one who had assimilated to Persian culture and told his niece not to reveal her identity. But now, the Bible tells us that Mordecai "told them he was a Jew" (Esther 3:4). Day after day, he refused to kneel before Haman, putting his very life at risk. In the following passage, the apostle Paul tells us how we likewise can stand strong even in the face of adversity.

> [13] *Therefore put on the full armor of God, so that when the day of evil comes, you may be able to stand your ground, and after you have done everything, to stand.* [14] *Stand firm then, with the belt of truth buckled around your waist, with the breastplate of righteousness in place,* [15] *and with your feet fitted with the readiness that comes from the gospel of peace.* [16] *In addition to all this, take up the shield of faith, with which you can extinguish all the flaming arrows of the evil one.* [17] *Take the helmet of salvation and the sword of the Spirit, which is the word of God (Ephesians 6:13–17).*

1. According to this passage, what allows you to stand your ground against the enemy?

2. Underline the different pieces of spiritual armor listed in this passage. Which pieces of armor do you feel confident you already have equipped? Why?

3. Which ones do you feel you need to equip? Why?

4. A Mordecai Moment could be just around the corner—an issue you haven't spoken up about, a part of yourself you've been hiding, an opportunity to change a person's life for the better. How could the full armor of God equip you to be prepared for it?

Prayer: *Heavenly Father, help me today to be strong in your mighty power. Equip me with each piece of your armor: the belt of truth, the breastplate of righteousness, my feet fitted with the readiness that comes from the gospel of peace, the shield of faith, and the helmet of salvation. And help me today to wield the sword of the Spirit, which is your Word.*

DAY 3: ESTHER EVENTS

Mordecai's change was radical—a complete reversal from his previous demeanor. But Esther's transformation was a bit more gradual. When Mordecai revealed to her the fate of the Jewish people, she was reluctant to approach King Xerxes. After all, her very life was at stake! When she did finally decide to act, she fasted for three days. Sometimes, we likewise need to wait before we take action. We need to plan our course and let our ideas simmer. We need to wait on the Lord's guidance. This is what Esther did—and it is what many others have done throughout the Bible. Read the following passages, and then answer the questions that follow.

> *"Go, gather together all the Jews who are in Susa, and fast for me. Do not eat or drink for three days, night or day. I and my attendants will fast as you do. When this is done, I will go to the king, even though it is against the law. And if I perish, I perish"* (Esther 4:16).

> [2] *Hanani, one of my brothers, came from Judah with some other men, and I questioned them about the Jewish remnant that had survived the exile, and also about Jerusalem.*

³ *They said to me, "Those who survived the exile and are back in the province are in great trouble and disgrace. The wall of Jerusalem is broken down, and its gates have been burned with fire."*

⁴ *When I heard these things, I sat down and wept. For some days I mourned and fasted and prayed before the God of heaven.* ⁵ *Then I said:*

"LORD, the God of heaven, the great and awesome God, who keeps his covenant of love with those who love him and keep his commandments, ⁶ *let your ear be attentive and your eyes open to hear the prayer your servant is praying before you day and night for your servants, the people of Israel. I confess the sins we Israelites, including myself and my father's family, have committed against you"* (Nehemiah 1:2–6).

²² *Immediately Jesus made the disciples get into the boat and go on ahead of him to the other side, while he dismissed the crowd.* ²³ *After he had dismissed them, he went up on a mountainside by himself to pray* (Matthew 14:22–23).

1. Have you ever made a decision too quickly or reacted to something when you should have taken more time to think and pray before responding? If so, what was the result?

2. Why did Esther, Nehemiah, and Jesus spend time alone fasting and praying?

3. Why do you think Jesus wanted to pray alone?

4. Is there anything currently in your life about which you need to pray or fast? If so, what do you feel like you should do before taking action?

Prayer: *Father, show me how to partner with you in your work of justice. May my words be measured and my actions careful. Please give me the strength to partner in this work that can be so hard and remind me to wait on you, to pause, to reflect, and to pray before I act. Bless these times of intentional prayer and fasting that I spend with you, and bring me clarity for my next step. Thank you for your guidance and wisdom.*

DAY 4: WHAT NOW?

During your group time this week, you considered areas of injustice within your own community. Jesus understood such injustice. He was poor, lived under Roman oppression in ancient Palestine, and was continually under attack by the religious establishment. Jesus understood injustice first-hand and fought against it. By reaching out to the marginalized, he set an example for how we can do the same. Read the following passage that relates one such example, when Jesus met a Samaritan woman at a well, and answer the questions that follow.

> [5] *So [Jesus] came to a town in Samaria called Sychar. . . .* [7] *When a Samaritan woman came to draw water, Jesus said to her, "Will you give me a drink?" . . .*
>
> [9] *The Samaritan woman said to him, "You are a Jew and I am a Samaritan woman. How can you ask me for a drink?" (For Jews do not associate with Samaritans.)*
>
> [10] *Jesus answered her, "If you knew the gift of God and who it is that asks you for a drink, you would have asked him and he would have given you living water."*
>
> [11] *"Sir," the woman said, "you have nothing to draw with and the well is deep. Where can you get this living water?* [12] *Are you greater than our father Jacob, who gave us the well and drank from it himself, as did also his sons and his livestock?"*
>
> [13] *Jesus answered, "Everyone who drinks this water will be thirsty again,* [14] *but whoever drinks the water I give them will never thirst. Indeed, the water I give them will become in them a spring of water welling up to eternal life"* (John 4:5–7, 9–14).

1. Who are the marginalized in your community? What are your interactions with them like?

2. According to John 4:9–10, what is the significance of Jesus' interacting with the Samaritan woman?

3. What does Jesus offer this woman? Why do you think he does this?

4. What does this conversation tell you about how you have been called to interact with the marginalized people in your world?

Prayer: *Lord, you are the God of the forgotten, the marginalized, and the outcast. You care about those whom society overlooks. The example you sent us in Jesus tells us that we are to care for those you care for and* *love those you loved. Help me to do this in my community. I can feel overwhelmed by the injustice against the marginalized around me. I don't know what to do or what my role should be. Give me a heart for your people. Give me the courage to offer them the living water of Jesus. And show me how I can. I pray this in Jesus' name. Amen.*

For next week, read chapters 6–7 in *You Were Made for This Moment.* Use the space below to note any key points or questions that you want to share at your next group meeting.

Heaven Set in Motion

(ESTHER 5:1–6:11)

WELCOME

Chance. Happenstance. The roll of the dice. This is often how life feels—just a series of random events and outcomes. But then there are those events and outcomes that seem to intersect with our lives not by *chance* but with great *purpose*. We meet a person who will become a great friend and mentor. We accept a job that takes us in an unexpected direction. We make a bold decision that opens the door to many new opportunities in the future.

Looking back, we realize these moments were not just a roll of the dice. They did not happen by chance or by accident. There was an Orchestrator behind them. Even the most skeptical among us recognizes this from time to time. Something divine was behind that meeting, or that opportunity, or that change of heart. There is just no way it was a coincidence.

This is what Esther and Mordecai experience in this next part of their story. The way the events unfold is beyond mere chance. God is behind these events—working in people's hearts, moving behind the scenes, conducting everything the way that he has planned. He is in the business of doing this. When we can't see a way out of our circumstances, he parts the waters and shows us a way to walk through on dry ground. When we don't know how to break down the walls, he causes them to fall. When we need a savior, he sends one in a miraculous way.

God is in the business of making the impossible possible. So, as you begin this session, consider the "impossible" situations that you are currently facing. What circumstance in your life right now desperately needs to change . . . but you can't imagine how it could? What in your life seems too big, too complicated, or too messy for anyone to handle?

As this session will reveal, the same God who saved his people in Esther's day is still in the business of saving his people today. He will set heaven in motion when we approach him in prayer—orchestrating events behind the scenes to move us into the place where he wants us to be. In the end, we find it's not the devil who is in the details. It's God!

SHARE

Take some time to share at least one key takeaway or insight you had from this week's personal studies. Then, to get things started, discuss one of the following questions:

- How do you explain the major turning points of your life? Was it fate, God's providence, or simply random events that brought them about?

— *or* —

- Have you ever experienced a miraculous event—
  something that could not be explained by chance
  or coincidence? If so, what happened?

READ

Ask one person to read the following passage, and then discuss the questions that follow.

> [28] And we know that in all things God works for the good of
> those who love him, who have been called according to his
> purpose. [29] For those God foreknew he also predestined to be
> conformed to the image of his Son, that he might be the first-
> born among many brothers and sisters. [30] And those he pre-
> destined, he also called; those he called, he also justified; those
> he justified, he also glorified (Romans 8:28–30).

According to this passage, for what purpose does God work
in our lives?

What role do you think God plays in the big and small events?

WATCH

Play the video teaching segment for session three (see the streaming video access provided on the inside front cover). As you watch, use the following outline to record any thoughts, questions, or points that stand out to you.

Esther's story was not just a rags-to-riches journey. Rather, her journey was from conformity to courage, from fear to faith, and—perhaps most important—from relying on herself and solving her own problems to relying on God and seeking his face.

The decisive moment in Esther's story didn't take place in the throne room of Xerxes. It took place in the throne room of heaven. She came before the king of Persia in beauty only after she lingered before the King of kings in humility.

We can't think for a moment that we have what it takes to weather this season of life. But we can't think for a second that God won't give us what we need.

God orchestrated all the details—the sleepless king, the detailed reading, the entry about Mordecai in the book, the entry of Haman in the castle court. God was at work even in the most pagan corner of the world.

Have you come to feel that even God is against you? Have you been led to believe that life is a roll of the dice—and you can't remember the last time they rolled in your favor? If so, ponder the plight of Haman and the outcome of Mordecai.

Always assume that God is at work. Move forward as if he is moving forward!

DISCUSS

Take a few minutes with your group members to discuss what you just heard and explore these concepts in Scripture.

1. Esther instructed all the Jews in Susa to pray and fast with her for three days. Why do you think she took this course of action prior to going before the king?

2. What does Esther's example reveal about the way we should approach the key decisions we need to make in our lives?

3. Read 1 Corinthians 1:27. How have you experienced clarity or breakthrough when you were in a state of weakness? What role did weakness play in getting you to that point?

4. Review Esther 6:1–11. What events led to Mordecai being exalted by the king?

5. What does this tell you about how God intervenes in our lives and on our behalf?

6. Do you believe God is in the details of your life? Why or why not?

RESPOND

Draw a timeline in the space below of the last decade of your life. Mark any major events that took place. Place a star beside any event that you believe was God ordained. Break into pairs and share your timelines with one another.

PRAY

Spend some time praying through your timelines. Rejoice over the God-ordained events and thank him for helping you get through the losses and disappointments. Pray for the unknowns, the difficult circumstances you are facing, and the questions for which you are currently waiting to receive answers. Thank the Lord for always ordering the steps of your life. Write down any prayer requests the group has, and pray for those needs during the coming week.

Personal Study

*R*eflect on the material you've covered this week by engaging in any or all of the following between-sessions activities. Each personal study consists of a passage of Scripture and reflection questions to help you dig deeper into this week's session. The time you invest will be well spent, so let God use it to draw you closer to him. At your next meeting, share any key points or insights that stood out to you as you spent this time with the Lord.

DAY 1: FINDING YOUR VOICE

In this session, we see Esther transform from a woman who was afraid to speak up to one who was courageous enough to enter the Persian king's throne room and ask for what she wanted. She had learned that her silence on the issue of her people and their impending extermination would be deadly. She could no longer just stand on the sidelines. Esther had found her voice. In the New Testament, we read that Mary also found strength in the Lord to use her "voice." Read her song, which she proclaimed after the angel of the Lord visited and told her that she would give birth to the Savior, and then answer the questions that follow.

> 46 *"My soul glorifies the Lord*
>   47 *and my spirit rejoices in God my Savior,*
> 48 *for he has been mindful*
>   *of the humble state of his servant.*
> *From now on all generations will call me blessed,*
>   49 *for the Mighty One has done great things for me—*
>   *holy is his name.*
> 50 *His mercy extends to those who fear him,*
>   *from generation to generation.*
> 51 *He has performed mighty deeds with his arm;*
>   *he has scattered those who are proud in their inmost thoughts.*
> 52 *He has brought down rulers from their thrones*
>   *but has lifted up the humble.*
> 53 *He has filled the hungry with good things*
>   *but has sent the rich away empty.*
> 54 *He has helped his servant Israel,*
>   *remembering to be merciful*
> 55 *to Abraham and his descendants forever,*
>   *just as he promised our ancestors"* (Luke 1:46–55).

1. When are you most hesitant to use your voice? Why?

2. What motivated Mary to sing these words?

3. How did she use her voice to address injustice?

4. How could Mary's song encourage you to speak up in your life or on behalf of others?

Prayer: *Father, I am often afraid to use my voice. I am afraid to speak up for myself and for others. I have believed the lie that my voice doesn't matter, that it doesn't count, that it's not strong enough. Tell me the truth about myself and my voice today—that it is strong, that it is enough, that it does count. Encourage me today. Help me to believe that my words are worth saying, especially when I know that they are from you.*

DAY 2: STRENGTH IN WEAKNESS

Christianity is full of paradoxes. "Blessed are the meek, for they will inherit the earth" (Matthew 5:5). "The last will be first, and the first will be last" (20:16). "I will not boast about myself, except about my weaknesses" (2 Corinthians 12:5). In a world that values power, grit, and determination, these ideas run counter-cultural. Yet what we see again and again in Scripture is God using people right in the midst of their weakness. He doesn't wait until they're strong. He doesn't wait until they're healed. He meets them where they are and uses them as they are. This is what he did with Esther. She was tired, hungry, and thirsty when she approached Xerxes' throne, yet this was the moment of her greatest strength. The apostle Paul found strength in weakness as well, as the following passage relates.

> *7 I was given a thorn in my flesh, a messenger of Satan, to torment me. 8 Three times I pleaded with the Lord to take it away from me. 9 But he said to me, "My grace is sufficient for you, for my power is made perfect in weakness." Therefore I will boast all the more gladly about my weaknesses, so that Christ's power may rest on me. 10 That is why, for Christ's sake, I delight in weaknesses, in insults, in hardships, in persecutions, in difficulties. For when I am weak, then I am strong* (2 Corinthians 12:7–10).

/ How do you feel about your own weaknesses? Do you tend to run from them, feel ashamed of them, or embrace them? Explain your response.

2. How did God answer Paul's prayer to take the "thorn," his difficulty, away from him?

3. Why did Paul "delight in weakness"?

4. What is a thorn in your side today? How could God use this weakness to display his strength either within you or to others?

Prayer: *Heavenly Father, thank you for the promise that your grace is sufficient to meet me in my time of weakness. Thank you for demonstrating your power within me during moments of need. Today, I pray that I will always look first to you, to your strength, and to your guidance instead of trying to meet my needs in my own power.*

DAY 3: GOD IS IN THE DETAILS

As you discussed this week in your group, the events leading to Mordecai's recognition by the king could only have been orchestrated by God. Everyone had to be in the right place at the right time for such a reversal of fates to occur—for Haman, who wanted to execute Mordecai, to end up planning a parade for him instead. It's easy to recognize the hand of God in stories like this. But it's harder to recognize the hand of God in our own lives, especially when heartbreak, tragedy, and confusion seem to be around every corner. We may wonder if God is really in the details—or is it the devil after all? Read the following passages of what the Bible has to say about how God intervenes in our lives, and then answer the questions that follow.

> [103] *How sweet are your words to my taste,*
>   *sweeter than honey to my mouth!*
> [104] *I gain understanding from your precepts;*
>   *therefore I hate every wrong path.*
> [105] *Your word is a lamp for my feet,*
>   *a light on my path* (Psalm 119:103–105).

> *In their hearts humans plan their course, but the LORD establishes their steps* (Proverbs 16:9).

> [28] *And we know that in all things God works for the good of those who love him, who have been called according to his purpose.* [29] *For those God foreknew he also predestined to be conformed to the image of his Son, that he might be the firstborn among many brothers and sisters.* [30] *And those he predestined, he also called; those he called, he also justified; those he justified, he also glorified* (Romans 8:28–30).

1. Do see God at work in your life today? Why or why not?

2. According to these verses, how does God interact with you? How does he speak to you?

3. According to Romans 8:28–30, what is God's plan for anyone who is in Christ Jesus?

4. What do you think about God's plan for your life in this season? Do you feel like you know what he wants for you, or is it unclear? Explain your answer.

Prayer: *Lord, be a lamp unto my feet and a light unto my path. Speak to me through your Word, through prayer, and through the wisdom of trusted friends. I'm not always sure where my life is headed. I don't always see how my circumstances could be turned around. But you make a way where there seems to be no way. Help me trust in that way and not my own. Thank you that your ultimate plan for me has already been fulfilled through the life-saving blood of Jesus.*

DAY 4: THE LORD WILL FIGHT FOR YOU

It is likely that Mordecai never thought that he would get the recognition he deserved for the good deed he had done in revealing the assassination plot against Xerxes. On the other hand, Haman fully believed he deserved recognition from the king for the evil he had plotted. But God had other plans, and he set heaven in motion to flip the stories of the two men. Perhaps you likewise are waiting for the recognition you deserve for the good you have done. You've watched as those around you have been recognized—perhaps for things they didn't deserve—and you wonder if your turn will ever come. But the Bible reveals that *God* knows. He knows your heart, sees your integrity, and fights for you, as the following passages relate.

> [13] *"Do not be afraid. Stand firm and you will see the deliverance the* Lord *will bring you today. The Egyptians you see today you will never see again.* [14] *The* Lord *will fight for you; you need only to be still"* (Exodus 14:13–14).

> *This is what the* Lord *says to you: "Do not be afraid or discouraged because of this vast army. For the battle is not yours, but God's"* (2 Chronicles 20:15).

> [15] *So people will be brought low*
>   *and everyone humbled,*
>   *the eyes of the arrogant humbled.*
> [16] *But the* Lord *Almighty will be exalted by his justice,*
>   *and the holy God will be proved holy by his righteous acts*
> (Isaiah 5:15–16).

² *"So when you give to the needy, do not announce it with trumpets, as the hypocrites do in the synagogues and on the streets, to be honored by others. Truly I tell you, they have received their reward in full. ³ But when you give to the needy, do not let your left hand know what your right hand is doing, ⁴ so that your giving may be in secret. Then your Father, who sees what is done in secret, will reward you"* (Matthew 6:2–4).

1. Have you ever done a good deed or accomplished something significant without recognition? How did it feel? What kind of recognition did you think you deserved?

2. How does God fight for you? What has this looked like in your life?

3. How is God described in Isaiah 5:15–16? What does this tell you about how God judges the motives of people's hearts?

4. What does Jesus say in Matthew 6:2–4 that your mind-set should be when you do a good deed or help a person in need? How easy or difficult is this for you to do?

Prayer: *Dear God, the battles I try to fight for myself are not mine but yours. Remind me of this truth whenever I try to prove my own value, or defend my integrity, or when I don't receive the recognition for the work that I have done. Continually remind me that you are fighting for me, that you are just, and that in the end all will be right. For only you are truly righteous, holy, and good. Keep these truths in my heart today, Father. In Jesus' name I pray. Amen.*

For next week, read chapters 8–9 in *You Were Made for This Moment.* Use the space below to note any key points or questions that you want to share at your next group meeting.

The God of Great Turnarounds

(ESTHER 6:12–9:1)

WELCOME

Have you experienced a dramatic turnaround in your life? Your flight was canceled for bad weather, but the airline found another one for you at the same time . . . and gave you an upgrade. The cleaners wrecked one of your shirts but ended up replacing it with a better one. A friend you thought was mad at you calls out of the blue and apologizes for the misunderstanding.

Our days, and our lives, can go from gloomy to sunny in a moment.

In this session, you will witness the great turnaround that occurs in the lives of Esther, Mordecai, and the Jews living in Persia. A doomed fate is suddenly transformed into a hopeful future. A nameless civil servant is suddenly donning a crown. A villain's identity was finally revealed, a heartless king grows a heart, and an entire people's death sentence is wiped away. It is the type of turnaround that only God can perform.

While canceled flights, wrecked shirts, and disagreements with friends all matter in their own ways, the turnarounds we really need are with the bigger things in life—our health, kids, futures, and finances. When these are going in the wrong direction, it's hard to imagine how things could turn around. But at these times, we must remember that our battle is not with our circumstances, or our boss, or our bank account. The real battle is not one of flesh and blood or one that is tangible at all. As Paul wrote, "Our struggle is not against flesh and blood, but against the rulers, against the authorities, against the powers of this dark world and against the spiritual forces of evil in the heavenly realms" (Ephesians 6:12).

If our problems are spiritual, it means the solutions to those problems are spiritual as well. God does not expect us to find our own way out of a powerless situation. He does not expect us to work a miracle, to change someone's heart, or even to change our own. God is the God of great turnarounds, and he can do what we consider to be impossible. As this next part of Esther's story reveals, there is no situation that he cannot turn around for the good.

SHARE

Take some time to share at least one key takeaway or insight you had from this week's personal studies. Then, to get things started, discuss one of the following questions:

- When was the last time you experienced a turnaround that changed a bad day into a good one? What turned things around?

— or —

- Haman and Mordecai getting what they deserved provides us with a sense of "poetic justice." When have you experienced this type of justice in your life?

READ

Ask one person to read the following passage, and then discuss the questions that follow.

> [10] *Finally, be strong in the Lord and in his mighty power.* [11] *Put on the full armor of God, so that you can take your stand against the devil's schemes.* [12] *For our struggle is not against flesh and blood, but against the rulers, against the authorities, against the powers of this dark world and against the spiritual forces of evil in the heavenly realms* (Ephesians 6:10–12).

What does it mean to be "strong in the Lord" and in "his mighty power"?

Paul says we don't battle against flesh and blood but against authorities and unseen powers. How could knowing this help reframe what you're struggling with right now?

WATCH

Play the video segment for session four (see the streaming video access provided on the inside front cover). As you watch, use the following outline to record any thoughts, questions, or points that stand out to you.

Haman, who wanted to kill a Jew for not falling down in his presence, was caught falling down before a Jew. Don't you love the ironies in this story?

Our God is a just God. Nothing escapes him.

When we pray, we engage the power of God against the devil. When we worship, we do what Satan himself did not do: we place God on the throne.

Do Hamans and Hitlers, lynch mobs and vigilantes, get away with murder? The Bible's answer is a resounding *no*!

The day is coming when God will forever balance the scales of justice. Until then, you and I are to partner with him in the pursuit of what is right.

Keep employing the weapons of prayer and worship. Keep trusting God. Your story is not finished. You may be just a day away from a game-changing turnaround.

DISCUSS

Take a few minutes with your group members to discuss what you just heard and explore these concepts in Scripture.

1. Read Esther 7:3–4. How do you think Esther felt in this moment? What risk was she taking? Why was she willing to take it?

2. What does Haman's fate tell you about the character of God?

3. Do you personally believe this about God? Why or why not?

4. What Haman-like situation in your life are you waiting for God to resolve? What has this waiting felt like for you?

5. What are you called to do while we wait on the Lord's justice? What does—or could—this look like in your own life?

6. How did the Jews' fate change in this part of our story? What does this tell you about the potential for your Haman-like situation to turn around?

RESPOND

Return to the Respond section that you completed in session two and give any updates to the group. Have you found a way to partner in God's work of justice in your community? If so, how? If not, what obstacles are you facing? How could you work together to overcome them? Write down one or two action items that could help you make progress this week.

PRAY

Have someone from the group close your time in prayer, thanking God for the turnarounds that he has already brought into your lives and asking him to continue to work in the situations where a turnaround is still needed. Write down any prayer requests the group has, and pray for those needs during the coming week.

Personal Study

*R*eflect on the material you've covered this week by engaging in any or all of the following between-sessions activities. Each personal study consists of a passage of Scripture and reflection questions to help you dig deeper into this week's session. The time you invest will be well spent, so let God use it to draw you closer to him. At your next meeting, share any key points or insights that stood out to you as you spent this time with the Lord.

DAY 1: A SPIRITUAL BATTLE

When the world is filled with Hamans—the Haman of violence, the Haman of sickness, the Haman of racism—it's easy to get discouraged. We in our human power can do only so much. Still, we tend to rely on our human power to fix, solve, and resolve the problems around us and within us. As you learned in this week's session, our battle is not one of flesh and blood "but against the rulers, against the authorities, against the powers of this dark world and against the spiritual forces of evil in the heavenly realms" (Ephesians 6:12). If that battle is between spiritual forces, why not use spiritual forces to fight for victory? Why continue relying on our own strength, willpower, and ideas when we have access to the throne room of God? Read the following verses about the power of prayer and answer the questions below.

> [12] *"Very truly I tell you, whoever believes in me will do the works I have been doing, and they will do even greater things than these, because I am going to the Father. [13] And I will do whatever you ask in my name, so that the Father may be glorified in the Son. [14] You may ask me for anything in my name, and I will do it"* (John 14:12–14).

> [6] *Do not be anxious about anything, but in every situation, by prayer and petition, with thanksgiving, present your requests to God. [7] And the peace of God, which transcends all understanding, will guard your hearts and your minds in Christ Jesus* (Philippians 4:6–7).

> [18] *And pray in the Spirit on all occasions with all kinds of prayers and requests. With this in mind, be alert and always keep on praying for all the Lord's people* (Ephesians 6:18).

1. In John 14:12–14, what does Jesus say is possible when you believe in him?

2. What does Jesus say that he will do when you petition the Father in his name?

3. What does Paul advise in Philippians 4:6–7 and Ephesians 6:18 about the type of requests to make to God? How often and at what times should you pray?

4. After studying these passages, how could you balance action with prayer regarding the "Haman" that you are facing today?

Prayer: *Heavenly Father, thank you for the promise in your Word that you hear me when I pray. There are so many Hamans right now in my life—so many situations beyond my control. I need a turnaround that only you can orchestrate. Today, I want to make all my requests known to you—holding nothing back—trusting that you can accomplish even what seems impossible.*

DAY 2: A PLOT TWIST

One of the greatest stories in the Bible about God orchestrating a turnaround occurs in the life of Joseph. He was shunned by his brothers. When Joseph was young, they threw him into a pit and sold him to slave traders headed for Egypt. Joseph ended up in the household of a powerful man but was soon thrown into prison for a crime he didn't commit. He was freed when he was summoned to interpret Pharaoh's dream about a widespread famine that was coming. Because of this dream, Pharaoh hired Joseph to lead a nationwide effort to store food—the very food that would lure Joseph's brothers into Egypt. By the time Joseph again saw his brothers, he was the second-most powerful man in the country. However, as the following passage relates, Joseph was not bitter toward them but understood why all these trials had come to pass.

> [15] When Joseph's brothers saw that their father was dead, they said, "What if Joseph holds a grudge against us and pays us back for all the wrongs we did to him?" [16] So they sent word to Joseph, saying, "Your father left these instructions before he died: [17] 'This is what you are to say to Joseph: I ask you to forgive your brothers the sins and the wrongs they committed in treating you so badly.' Now please forgive the sins of the servants of the God of your father." When their message came to him, Joseph wept.
>
> [18] His brothers then came and threw themselves down before him. "We are your slaves," they said.
>
> [19] But Joseph said to them, "Don't be afraid. Am I in the place of God? [20] You intended to harm me, but God

intended it for good to accomplish what is now being done, the saving of many lives. [21] So then, don't be afraid. I will provide for you and your children." And he reassured them and spoke kindly to them (Genesis 50:15–21).

1. What did Joseph's brothers fear when their father died?

2. What did the brothers do to protect themselves from any bitterness on Joseph's part?

3. What did Joseph say was the purpose for the series of unfortunate events that befell him in his life? What do you think of this reasoning?

4. How do you find hope in Joseph's story for your own needed turnaround?

Prayer: *Dear God, you know the struggles I've faced. You know the path I am on. You know my life has not gone the way I had hoped. I confess that I've often wondered where you are in the midst of my pain. I wonder if you care. I wonder if you're able to change my circumstances. Thank you for the example of Joseph and so many others in Scripture. I know that just as you work miracles in their lives, you can work them in mine too. Do the work only you can do. Change what only you can change—and give me hope and belief that you will. In Jesus' name I pray. Amen.*

DAY 3: THE GREATEST REVERSAL OF ALL

The greatest plot twist of all happened in Jesus' life, death, and resurrection. Jesus was the incarnation of God, born to a humble family. During his ministry, he became a powerful teacher with thousands of followers. By the end of his time on earth, he was a convicted man with a Roman death sentence. Then the greatest turnaround of all happened. Read the following story of this turnaround, found in John's Gospel, and then answer the questions that follow.

> [11] *Now Mary stood outside the tomb crying. As she wept, she bent over to look into the tomb* [12] *and saw two angels in white, seated where Jesus' body had been, one at the head and the other at the foot.*
>
> [13] *They asked her, "Woman, why are you crying?"*
>
> *"They have taken my Lord away," she said, "and I don't know where they have put him."* [14] *At this, she turned around and saw Jesus standing there, but she did not realize that it was Jesus.*

¹⁵ *He asked her, "Woman, why are you crying? Who is it you are looking for?"*

Thinking he was the gardener, she said, "Sir, if you have carried him away, tell me where you have put him, and I will get him."

¹⁶ *Jesus said to her, "Mary."*

She turned toward him and cried out in Aramaic, "Rabboni!" (which means "Teacher").

¹⁷ *Jesus said, "Do not hold on to me, for I have not yet ascended to the Father. Go instead to my brothers and tell them, 'I am ascending to my Father and your Father, to my God and your God.'"*

¹⁸ *Mary Magdalene went to the disciples with the news: "I have seen the Lord!" And she told them that he had said these things to her* (John 20:11–18).

1. What is the greatest tragedy you have faced in your life? How did this event affect you?

2. How was Mary feeling at the beginning of this passage? Why was she feeling this way?

3. When did Mary realize she was talking to Jesus? What do you think went through her mind when she realized she was talking to the risen Christ?

4. How could this story give you hope in the midst of tragedy—whether that is a tragedy you are facing now or one that you have faced in the past?

Prayer: *Lord, remind me that sadness, grief, and tragedy are not the end of the story. If you are capable of resurrection, you are capable of resurrecting what has died in my own life. You can make all things new. You can turn my mourning into dancing. You can move through grief with me until I find joy. Because of the truth of the resurrection, I believe in the resurrecting power you have over my life. Thank you, Jesus, for this miracle in my life.*

DAY 4: WHILE WE WAIT

God can make the greatest of turnarounds happen in our lives, but rarely do they happen overnight. More likely, they occur over the course of a week, a month, a year, or even longer. This begs the question: *what do we do while we're waiting for the turnaround we so desperately need?* As you heard in this week's teaching, one thing you can do as you wait is to partner with God "in the pursuit of what is right." But how do we do this? Read the following parable of the Good Samaritan for some clues and answer the questions that follow.

²⁵ On one occasion an expert in the law stood up to test Jesus. "Teacher," he asked, "what must I do to inherit eternal life?"

²⁶ "What is written in the Law?" he replied. "How do you read it?"

²⁷ He answered, "'Love the Lord your God with all your heart and with all your soul and with all your strength and with all your mind'; and, 'Love your neighbor as yourself.'"

²⁸ "You have answered correctly," Jesus replied. "Do this and you will live."

²⁹ But he wanted to justify himself, so he asked Jesus, "And who is my neighbor?"

³⁰ In reply Jesus said: "A man was going down from Jerusalem to Jericho, when he was attacked by robbers. They stripped him of his clothes, beat him and went away, leaving him half dead. ³¹ A priest happened to be going down the same road, and when he saw the man, he passed by on the other side. ³² So too, a Levite, when he came to the place and saw him, passed by on the other side.

³³ But a Samaritan, as he traveled, came where the man was; and when he saw him, he took pity on him. ³⁴ He went to him and bandaged his wounds, pouring on oil and wine. Then he put the man on his own donkey, brought him to an inn and took care of him. ³⁵ The next day he took out two denarii and gave them to the innkeeper. 'Look after him,' he

said, 'and when I return, I will reimburse you for any extra
expense you may have.'

³⁶ "Which of these three do you think was a neighbor to
the man who fell into the hands of robbers?"

³⁷ The expert in the law replied, "The one who had
mercy on him."

Jesus told him, "Go and do likewise" (Luke 10:25–37).

1. What questions from the expert in the law prompted
Jesus to tell this parable? According to Christ, how does
a person inherit eternal life?

2. Why did the priest and the Levite cross the road when
they saw the man in need?

3. There was a long history between the Jews and Samaritans, and the two groups did not get along. As John put
it, "Jews do not associate with Samaritans" (John 4:9).
But in this story, the one who finally helped the Jewish
man in need was a *Samaritan*. What is significant about
this? Why do you think Jesus included this detail?

4. When have you been like the priest and the Levite? When have you been a good Samaritan? How is God calling you to be a Good Samaritan to your neighbors this week?

Prayer: *Heavenly Father, I confess that at times I am guilty of judging other people. Help me today to see people the way that you see them. Help me to look beyond any differences that I might have with others and just reach out and serve them as Christ did for me. I want to be like the Good Samaritan in this story. Help me to continually make this my goal.*

For next week, read chapters 10–11 in *You Were Made for This Moment.* Use the space below to note any key points or questions that you want to share at your next group meeting.

Remembering God's Faithfulness

(ESTHER 9:2–10:3)

WELCOME

Pliny the Younger, a first-century Roman governor, made the following report to Emperor Trajan as it related to a particular practice among early Christians: "They were accustomed to meet on a fixed day before dawn and sing responsively a hymn to Christ as to a god, and to bind themselves by oath, not to do some crime, but not to commit fraud, theft, or adultery, not falsify their trust, nor to refuse to return a trust when called upon to do so. When this was over, it was their custom to depart and to assemble again to partake of food."

The Roman authorities were wondering about this new group who called themselves "Christians" and what exactly they did at these gatherings. Many people wonder the same of Christians today. Why do followers of Christ get together each week to talk about the same Scripture, the same God, and the same Savior . . . every Sunday?

If you're a churchgoer, you know why. Just think about Sunday morning compared to Monday morning. On Sunday, the message is fresh. The lyrics to a worship song are on your mind. Maybe you're a little more patient with your family or kinder to your neighbor. But then comes Monday. The alarm goes off early. You're rushing to get ready. Your kids can't find their homework and are complaining about having nothing to wear.

By the time you get to work, you're frazzled and irritated. So, you take it out on your coworker. You fire off an impatient email. All the warm fuzzy feelings from Sunday, the day before, are gone. Why? Because you've already forgotten the message, the worship, the scripture. Oh, how quickly we forget!

Mordecai knew how quickly his people would forget the work God had done to save them. So he instituted a holiday called Purim, still celebrated to this day, to mark the saving of the Jewish people from Haman. The story of Esther thus ends not with King Xerxes' edict but with a call to *remember*. In the same way, as you close out this study this week, it's important to remember what you've learned, to recall the faithfulness of God, and to let this season of learning be one to which you return in remembrance of God's goodness and provision.

SHARE

Take some time to share at least one key takeaway or insight you had from this week's personal studies. Then, to get things started, discuss one of the following questions:

- What kinds of ceremonies of remembrance do you celebrate? How do you participate in them? (This could include Christian holidays, such as Christmas and Easter, or be something personal to you or your family.)

— *or* —

• Why do you think it is so important to remember the acts of God's faithfulness in the past? What happens when we fail to remember?

READ

Ask one person to read the following passage, and then discuss the questions that follow.

> [23] *The Lord Jesus, on the night he was betrayed, took bread,* [24] *and when he had given thanks, he broke it and said, "This is my body, which is for you; do this in remembrance of me."* [25] *In the same way, after supper he took the cup, saying, "This cup is the new covenant in my blood; do this, whenever you drink it, in remembrance of me."* [26] *For whenever you eat this bread and drink this cup, you proclaim the Lord's death until he comes* (1 Corinthians 11:23–26).

What did Paul say was the purpose of partaking in communion or the Eucharist?

What does it mean to "proclaim the Lord's death until he comes"?

WATCH

Play the video for session five (see the streaming video access provided on the inside front cover). As you watch, use the following outline to record any thoughts, questions, or points that stand out to you.

Seasons of struggle can be treacherous for the human heart. When times are tough, we are sitting ducks for discouragement and defeat. Despair can be a dangerous season. But it can also be a developing time. Tough times can make us bitter or make us better.

Where God is small, problems are large. A wimpy God makes for a wimpy heart. But a great God makes for a solid saint. So let God be big. Believe that he is big!

We all suffer from spiritual amnesia. We forget that God can make beauty out of ashes, joy out of mourning, an army out of a valley of dead bones, and rejoicing out of sorrow.

The Christian version of the Persian miracle involves not Esther in Susa, but God's Son buried in a tomb. Just as Haman declared a death sentence on the Jews, so Satan declared a death sentence on the Source of life himself.

The God of great turnarounds performed his greatest work on Easter Sunday. And just so we would never forget this moment, Jesus gave us our own Purim celebration.

Never forget that the God of great turnarounds is the God who holds the future in his hands. For followers of Christ, the future is filled with victory from horizon to horizon.

DISCUSS

Take a few minutes with your group members to discuss what you just heard and explore these concepts in Scripture.

1. Read Esther 9:20–22. Why did Mordecai call his people to commemorate these days?

2. What is the significance of the word *Purim*?

3. How did this difficult season for the Jews make them better instead of bitter?

4. Read Luke 22:19–20. How does the celebration of Purim parallel the remembrance that Jesus called the disciples to observe during the Last Supper?

5. When has a difficult season made you better instead of bitter?

6. What do you remember about this time that gives you hope for a difficult season you're in now or could be sometime in the future?

RESPOND

Close this study by reflecting on the difficult seasons you have been through in the past year. How has God compelled you to step out of your comfort zone? What are some of the key decisions you have made? How have you seen God at work to create turnarounds in your story? What acts of his faithfulness do you most want to remember moving forward?

PRAY

Close your time in prayer, thanking God for the ways that he has led you during this study. Share any prayer requests and review how God has answered past prayers during the five weeks that you have met together. Use the space below to record any new requests, and be sure to pray for these needs and for your fellow group members in the coming week.

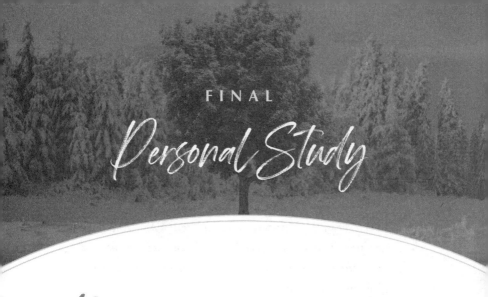

Personal Study

eflect on the material you've covered this final week by engaging in any or all of the following between-sessions activities. Each personal study consists of a passage of Scripture and reflection questions to help you dig deeper into this week's session. The time you invest will be well spent, so let God use it to draw you closer to him.

DAY 1: SHAPED FOR SPRINGTIME

The main characters in the book of Esther were strengthened through their trials. Mordecai stood up for what he believed. Esther found courage to approach the king. Both embraced their true identities as God's chosen people. But these changes were a product of suffering—of literally facing a death sentence. While no one enjoys suffering, some of the greatest changes we undergo in life happen as a result of it. We wouldn't be as strong, confident, loving, or secure without having gone through a dark and difficult time. Read the following passage in Romans about the value of suffering, and then answer the questions that follow.

¹ Therefore, since we have been justified through faith, we have peace with God through our Lord Jesus Christ, ² through whom we have gained access by faith into this grace in which we now stand. And we boast in the hope of the glory of God. ³ Not only so, but we also glory in our sufferings, because we know that suffering produces perseverance; ⁴ perseverance, character; and character, hope. ⁵ And hope does not put us to shame, because God's love has been poured out into our hearts through the Holy Spirit, who has been given to us (Romans 5:1–5).

1. What season of trial or suffering have you gone through that was transformative for you, your faith, and your relationships? How did you change as a result of that season in your life?

2. According to Paul's words in Romans 5:3–5, what does suffering produce? Has this been your experience? Explain your response.

3. What kind of hope does Paul promise in this passage?

4. How could a difficulty you are facing now produce perseverance? How could it produce character? How could it produce hope?

Prayer: *Dear God, I believe in your Word. I know it is true. I know it brings life. In the midst of my struggle, it can be hard to see how my suffering is developing perseverance, character, and hope within me. I want to believe this, but sometimes my suffering feels too great, too heavy, too dark. Give me the hope I need to get through this day. Remind me that good things happen in the waiting and the stillness. Show me how you've already cultivated perseverance and character in me, and fill me with hope that spring is coming. In Jesus' name. Amen.*

DAY 2: MAGNIFY THE LORD AND NOT THE PAIN

One way to ensure that our suffering will lead to character building and perseverance is to focus on God rather than on our pain. So often we think our problems are bigger than God's power, but if we learned anything from Esther's story, we know this is never the case. God was able to turn around the bleakest of circumstances, and he will do the same for you. In the meantime, let your troubles point you to the One who is greater than them. Read the following passages from Psalms about this truth, and then answer the questions that follow.

*¹ The L*ORD *is my shepherd, I lack nothing.*
² He makes me lie down in green pastures,
he leads me beside quiet waters,
³ he refreshes my soul.
He guides me along the right paths
for his name's sake.
⁴ Even though I walk
through the darkest valley,
I will fear no evil,
for you are with me;
your rod and your staff,
they comfort me (Psalm 23:1–4).

*The L*ORD *is my light and my salvation—*
whom shall I fear?
*The L*ORD *is the stronghold of my life—*
of whom shall I be afraid? (Psalm 27:1).

*Glorify the L*ORD *with me;*
let us exalt his name together (Psalm 34:3).

¹¹ The heavens are yours, and yours also the earth;
you founded the world and all that is in it.
¹² You created the north and the south;
Tabor and Hermon sing for joy at your name.
¹³ Your arm is endowed with power;
your hand is strong, your right hand exalted.
¹⁴ Righteousness and justice are the foundation of your throne;
love and faithfulness go before you (Psalm 89:11–14).

⁴ He determines the number of the stars
and calls them each by name.
⁵ Great is our Lord and mighty in power;
his understanding has no limit (Psalm 147:4–5).

1. Are there any problems, issues, or challenges in your life for which you find it difficult to rely on God? If so, which ones? Why?

2. Write down every word or phrase used to describe God in these passages. Which ones stand out to you? Why?

3. Why do you think the psalmists so often wrote of God's power?

4. According to these verses, what makes God capable of turning around the problems, issues, or challenges you wrote down above?

Prayer: *Heavenly Father, you are my light and my salvation. You are the stronghold of my life. I know that I have nothing to fear when I am walking with you, focusing on your goodness, for you shall lead me along* *the right paths, beside quiet waters, and through the darkest valleys. I declare that you are great and mighty in power. Make your presence known to me today.*

DAY 3: DO THIS IN REMEMBRANCE

We all live in cultures of remembrance. We celebrate certain holidays to commemorate momentous events. We celebrate anniversaries to remember the years we've been with our spouse. We get days off work to celebrate historical events. Culturally, it's important for us to remember our history and from where we came, as it helps us to understand who we are and where we're going. Remembrance, as we talked about during this week's session, is incredibly important to the Christian faith. We are called to remember not only who we are but who God is. Read the following passages about remembrance and answer the questions that follow.

> [10] *When the LORD your God brings you into the land he swore to your fathers, to Abraham, Isaac and Jacob, to give you—a land with large, flourishing cities you did not build,* [11] *houses filled with all kinds of good things you did not provide, wells you did not dig, and vineyards and olive groves you did not plant—then when you eat and are satisfied,* [12] *be careful that you do not forget the LORD, who brought you out of Egypt, out of the land of slavery (Deuteronomy 6:10–12).*

> [9] *Remember the former things, those of long ago;*
>   *I am God, and there is no other;*
>   *I am God, and there is none like me.*

^{10} *I make known the end from the beginning,*
from ancient times, what is still to come (Isaiah 46:9–10).

^{25} *"All this I have spoken while still with you.* ^{26} *But the Advocate, the Holy Spirit, whom the Father will send in my name, will teach you all things and will remind you of everything I have said to you.* ^{27} *Peace I leave with you; my peace I give you. I do not give to you as the world gives. Do not let your hearts be troubled and do not be afraid"* (John 14:25–27).

1. According to Deuteronomy 6:10–12 and Isaiah 46:9–10, what were the Israelites to remember about God?

2. Why do you think it was important for them to remember these things?

3. According to John 14:25–27, who will remind us of Jesus' teachings?

4. Have you experienced this in your life? If so, how?

Prayer: *Dear God, I confess that I have forgotten your power. I have forgotten your love. I have forgotten your wisdom. I know I have forgotten these things when I start to rely on myself for strength, discernment, and love. In you, I have all of these in abundance. Holy Spirit, remind me of this truth when I forget it. Remind me of the loving grace of my savior Jesus. Hold me in this remembrance—and may I hold it so that whatever I face, I have these memories of faithfulness to carry me through. In Christ's name I pray. Amen.*

DAY 4: FOR SUCH A TIME AS THIS

To close out your time in this study, review the following key passages from the book of Esther. You can then follow the question prompts below or journal whatever thoughts come to mind.

> *17 Now the king was attracted to Esther more than to any of the other women, and she won his favor and approval more than any of the other virgins. So he set a royal crown on her head and made her queen instead of Vashti. 18 And the king gave a great banquet, Esther's banquet, for all his nobles and officials. He proclaimed a holiday throughout the provinces and distributed gifts with royal liberality (Esther 2:17–18).*

²¹ *During the time Mordecai was sitting at the king's gate, Bigthana and Teresh, two of the king's officers who guarded the doorway, became angry and conspired to assassinate King Xerxes.* ²² *But Mordecai found out about the plot and told Queen Esther, who in turn reported it to the king, giving credit to Mordecai* (Esther 2:21–22).

¹ *After these events, King Xerxes honored Haman son of Hammedatha, the Agagite, elevating him and giving him a seat of honor higher than that of all the other nobles.* ² *All the royal officials at the king's gate knelt down and paid honor to Haman, for the king had commanded this concerning him. But Mordecai would not kneel down or pay him honor* (Esther 3:1–2).

¹ *When Mordecai learned of all that had been done, he tore his clothes, put on sackcloth and ashes, and went out into the city, wailing loudly and bitterly.* ² *But he went only as far as the king's gate, because no one clothed in sackcloth was allowed to enter it. . . .*

⁹ *Hathak went back and reported to Esther what Mordecai had said.* ¹⁰ *Then she instructed him to say to Mordecai,* ¹¹ *"All the king's officials and the people of the royal provinces know that for any man or woman who approaches the king in the inner court without being summoned the king has but one law: that they be put to death unless the king extends the gold scepter to them and spares their lives. But thirty days have passed since I was called to go to the king."*

¹² *When Esther's words were reported to Mordecai,* ¹³ *he sent back this answer: "Do not think that because you are in the king's house you alone of all the Jews will escape.* ¹⁴ *For if*

you remain silent at this time, relief and deliverance for the Jews will arise from another place, but you and your father's family will perish. And who knows but that you have come to your royal position for such a time as this?" (Esther 4:1–2, 9–14).

¹⁵ Then Esther sent this reply to Mordecai: ¹⁶ "Go, gather together all the Jews who are in Susa, and fast for me. Do not eat or drink for three days, night or day. I and my attendants will fast as you do. When this is done, I will go to the king, even though it is against the law. And if I perish, I perish" (Esther 4:15–16).

¹ That night the king could not sleep; so he ordered the book of the chronicles, the record of his reign, to be brought in and read to him. ² It was found recorded there that Mordecai had exposed Bigthana and Teresh, two of the king's officers who guarded the doorway, who had conspired to assassinate King Xerxes.

³ "What honor and recognition has Mordecai received for this?" the king asked.

"Nothing has been done for him," his attendants answered (Esther 6:1–3).

¹ So the king and Haman went to Queen Esther's banquet, ² and as they were drinking wine on the second day, the king again asked, "Queen Esther, what is your petition? It will be given you. What is your request? Even up to half the kingdom, it will be granted."

³ Then Queen Esther answered, "If I have found favor with you, Your Majesty, and if it pleases you, grant me my life—this is my petition. And spare my people—this is my request. ⁴ For I and my people have been sold to be destroyed, killed and annihilated. If we had merely been sold as male and female slaves, I would have kept quiet, because no such distress would justify disturbing the king."

⁵ King Xerxes asked Queen Esther, "Who is he? Where is he—the man who has dared to do such a thing?"

⁶ Esther said, "An adversary and enemy! This vile Haman!" (Esther 7:1-6).

¹¹ The king's edict granted the Jews in every city the right to assemble and protect themselves; to destroy, kill and annihilate the armed men of any nationality or province who might attack them and their women and children, and to plunder the property of their enemies. ¹² The day appointed for the Jews to do this in all the provinces of King Xerxes was the thirteenth day of the twelfth month, the month of Adar (Esther 8:11-12).

²⁰ Mordecai recorded these events, and he sent letters to all the Jews throughout the provinces of King Xerxes, near and far, ²¹ to have them celebrate annually the fourteenth and fifteenth days of the month of Adar ²² as the time when the Jews got relief from their enemies, and as the month when their sorrow was turned into joy and their mourning into a day of celebration. He wrote them to observe the days as days of feasting and joy and giving presents of food to one another and gifts to the poor (Esther 9:20-22).

1. What did you learn about God's character from this study?

2. What did you learn about yourself?

3. What is the most significant point that stands out to you from this study?

4. Has this study helped reveal how God has made you for the time and place you live in? If so, how have you been made for this moment?

Prayer: *Lord, thank you for bringing me to this story of Esther when I needed it. Thank you for what I have learned about you, Jesus, and myself. May I carry these lessons with me as I face struggles, difficulties, and the unknown. When I am in a winter season, may I remember the lives of Esther and Mordecai. May I draw strength from the victory they found in you. May I remember that your guidance and delivery were not just for them; they were for me too. Thank you for being the God of great turnarounds. Thank you for being the God of justice. May you guide me as I partner with you in the work you have for me. In Jesus' name. Amen.*

Leader's Guide

Thank you for your willingness to lead your group through this study! What you have chosen to do is valuable and will make a great difference in the lives of others. The rewards of being a leader are different from those who are participating, and we hope that as you lead you will find your own walk with Jesus deepened by this experience.

You Were Made for This Moment is a five-session study built around video content and small group interaction. As a group leader, think of yourself as the host. Your job is to take care of your guests by managing the behind-the-scenes details so that when everyone arrives, they can enjoy their time together. As the leader, your job is not to answer all the questions or reteach the content—the video, book, and study guide will do that work. Your job is to guide the experience and cultivate your small group into a kind of teaching community. This will make it a place for members to process, question, and reflect—not receive more instruction.

Before your first meeting, make sure everyone in the group gets a copy of the study guide. This will keep everyone on the same page and help the process run more smoothly. If some group members are unable to purchase the guide, arrange it so that people can share the resource with other group members. Giving everyone access to all the material will position this study to be as rewarding an experience as possible. Everyone should feel free to write in his or her study guide and bring it to group every week.

WEEKLY PREPARATION

As the group leader, there are a few things you should do to prepare for each meeting:

- *Read through the session.* This will help you to become more familiar with the content and know how to structure the discussion times.

- *Decide which questions you definitely want to discuss.* Based on the amount and length of group discussion, you may not be able to get through all the questions, so choose four to five that you definitely want to cover.

- *Be familiar with the questions you want to discuss.* When the group meets you'll be watching the clock, so you want to make sure you are familiar with the questions you have selected. In this way, you'll ensure you have the material more deeply in your mind than your group members.

- *Pray for your group.* Pray for your group members throughout the week and ask God to lead them as they study his Word.

In many cases, there will be no one "right" answer to the question. Answers will vary, especially when the group members are being asked to share their personal experiences.

SETTING UP THE GROUP

You will need to determine with your group how long you want to meet each week so you can plan your time accordingly. Generally, most groups like to meet from one to two hours, so you could use one of the following schedules:

SECTION	60 MIN.	90 MIN.	120 MIN.
WELCOME (members arrive and get settled)	5 min	5 min	10 min
SHARE & READ (discuss the icebreaker questions)	10 min	15 min	15 min
WATCH (watch the video teaching)	15 min	15 min	15 min
DISCUSS (discuss the group questions)	25 min	40 min	60 min
RESPOND & PRAY (close the group time)	5 min	15 min	20 min

As the group leader, you will want to create an environment that encourages sharing and learning. A church sanctuary or formal classroom may not be as ideal as a living room, because those locations can feel formal and less intimate. No matter what setting you choose, provide enough comfortable seating for everyone, and, if possible, arrange the seats in a semi-circle so everyone can see the video easily. This will make the transition between the video and the group conversation more efficient and natural.

Also, try to get to the meeting site early so you can greet participants as they arrive. Simple refreshments create a welcoming atmosphere and can be a wonderful addition to a group study evening. Try to take food and pet allergies into account to make your guests as comfortable as possible. You may also want to consider offering childcare for couples with children who want to attend. Finally, be sure your media technology is working properly. Managing these details up front will make the rest of your group experience flow smoothly and provide a welcoming space in which to engage the content of *You Were Made for This Moment*.

STARTING THE GROUP TIME

Once everyone has arrived, it is time to begin the group. Here are some simple tips to make your group time healthy, enjoyable, and effective. First, begin the meeting with a short prayer and remind the group members to put their phones on silent. This is a way to make sure you can all be present with one another and with God. Next, facilitate the "Share" and "Read" questions using the directions provided in this study guide. Note that this won't require as much time in session one, but beginning in session two, you may need to allow for more time if people also want to share any insights from their personal studies.

LEADING THE DISCUSSION TIME

Now that the group is engaged, watch the video and respond with some directed small-group discussion. Encourage the group members to participate in the discussion, but make sure they know they don't have to do so. As the discussion progresses, follow up with comments such as, "Tell me more about that," or, "Why did you answer that way?" This will allow the group participants to deepen their reflections and invite meaningful sharing in a nonthreatening way.

Although there are six discussion questions for each session, you do not have to use them all or even follow them in order. Feel free to pick and choose the questions based on either the needs of your group or how the conversation is flowing. Also, don't be afraid of silence. Offering a question and allowing up to thirty seconds of silence is okay. It allows people space to think about how they want to respond and also gives them time to do so.

As group leader, you are the boundary keeper for your group. Do not let anyone (yourself included) dominate the group time. Keep an eye out for group members who might be tempted to "attack" folks they disagree with or try to "fix" those having struggles. These kinds of behaviors can derail a group's momentum, so they need to be steered in a different direction. Model active listening and encourage everyone in your group to do the same. This will make your group time a safe space and create a positive community.

GROUP DYNAMICS

Leading a group through the *You Were Made for This Moment Study Guide* will prove to be highly rewarding. However, this doesn't mean that you will not encounter any challenges along the way! Discussions can get off track. Group members may not be sensitive to the needs and ideas of others. Some might worry they will be expected to talk about matters that make them feel awkward. Others may express comments that result in disagreements. To help ease this strain on you and the group, consider the following ground rules:

- When someone raises a question or comment that is off topic, suggest you deal with it another time, or, if you feel led to go in that direction, let the group know you will be spending some time discussing it.

- If someone asks a question you don't know how to answer, admit it and move on. At your discretion, feel free to invite group members to comment on questions that call for personal experience.

- If you find one or two people are dominating the discussion time, direct a few questions to others in the group. Outside the main group time, ask the more dominating members to help you draw out the quieter ones. Work to make them a part of the solution instead of the problem.

- When a disagreement occurs, encourage the group members to process the matter in love.

- Encourage those on opposite sides to restate what they heard the other side say about the matter, and then invite each side to evaluate if that perception is accurate. Lead the group in examining other passages of Scripture related to the topic and look for common ground.

When any of these issues arise, encourage your group members to follow these words from the Bible: "Love one another" (John 13:34), "If it is possible, as far as it depends on you, live at peace with everyone" (Romans 12:18), "Whatever is true . . . noble . . . right . . . if anything is excellent or praiseworthy—think about such things" (Philippians 4:8), and "Be quick to listen, slow to speak and slow to become angry" (James 1:19). This will make your group time more rewarding and beneficial for everyone who attends.

CLOSING YOUR GROUP TIME

The group discussion leads to a closing time of reflection and prayer. During this time, encourage the participants to review what they have learned and share any needs they have with the group. Close your time by taking a few minutes to pray for those needs and to record any prayer requests that the group members have for the upcoming week. Beginning in session two, be sure to check in regarding these requests and see how God has answered them.

At the end of each session, invite the group members to complete the between-sessions personal study for that week. If you so choose, explain you will provide some time before the video teaching next week for anyone to share insights. Let them know sharing is optional, and it's not a problem if they can't get to the between-sessions activities some weeks. It will still be beneficial for them to hear from the other participants and learn about what they discovered.

Thank you again for taking the time to lead your group. You are making a difference in the lives of others and having an impact on the kingdom of God.

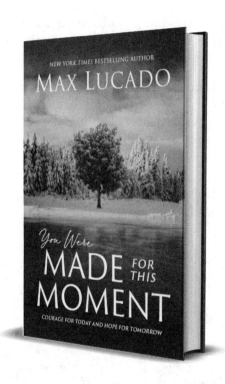

Study Books of the Bible with Trusted Pastors

The 40 Days Through the Book series has been designed to help believers more actively engage with God's Word. Each study encourages participants to read through one book in the New Testament at least once during the course of 40 days and provides them with:

- A clear understanding of the background and culture in which the book was written,
- Insights into key passages of Scripture, and
- Clear applications and takeaways from the particular book that participants can apply to their lives.

Available now at your favorite bookstore, or streaming video on StudyGateway.com.

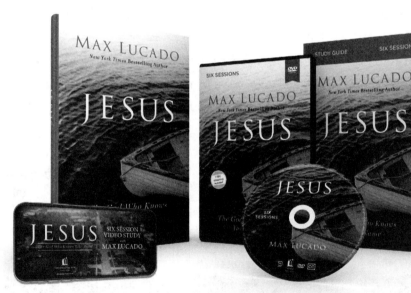

CELEBRATE EASTER, CHRISTMAS, AND THE LIFE AND MINISTRY OF JESUS

In *Because of Bethlehem*, a four-session video Bible study, Max Lucado explores how the One who made everything chose to make himself nothing and come into our world. Jesus' birth gives us the promise that God is always near us, always for us, and always within us—and that we no longer need to have marks on our record.

In *He Chose the Nails*, a five-session video Bible study, Max continues by examining the gifts that Christ gave at his crucifixion. These include not only the gift of the cross but also the gift of the thorns, the nails, and the empty tomb. The cross is rich with God's gifts of grace, and as we unwrap them, we will hear him whisper, "I did it just for you."

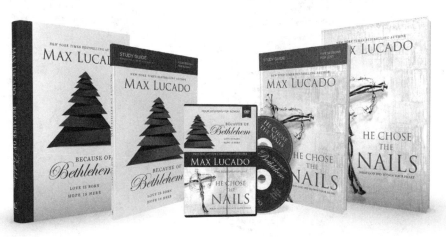

Book	Christmas Study Guide	DVD	Easter Study Guide	Book
9780849947599	9780310687054	9780310687849	9780310687269	9780718085070

Available now at your favorite bookstore,
or streaming video on StudyGateway.com.

GOD HAS A CURE FOR YOUR WORRIES

Anxiety doesn't have to dominate life. Max looks at seven admonitions from the Apostle Paul in Philippians 4:4–8 that lead to one wonderful promise: "The peace of God which surpasses all understanding." He shows how God is ready to give comfort to help us face the calamities in life, view bad news through the lens of sovereignty, discern the lies of Satan, and tell ourselves the truth. We can discover true peace from God that surpasses all human understanding.

Study Guide
9780310087311

DVD
9780310087335

Softcover
9780718074210

Available now at your favorite bookstore,
or streaming video on StudyGateway.com.

HarperChristian Resources

THAT ALWAYS DELIVERS

In this book and video Bible study, Max Lucado shares the unexpected path to a lasting happiness, one that produces reliable joy in any season of life. Based on the teachings of Jesus and backed by modern research, *How Happiness Happens* presents a surprising but practical way of living that will change you from the inside out.

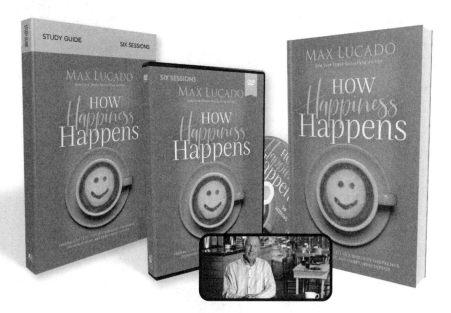

Study Guide	DVD with Free Streaming Access	Book
9780310105718	9780310105732	9780718096137

Available now at your favorite bookstore,
or streaming video on StudyGateway.com.

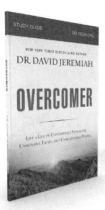
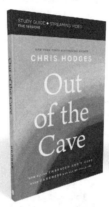
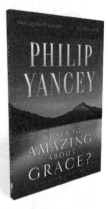